SUMMONS

MARQUAVIOUS MOORE

First published by Marquavious Moore 2024
Copyright © 2024 by Marquavious Moore
All rights reserved. No part of this publication may be reproduced, stored or transmitted in any form or by any means, electronic, mechanical, photocopying, recording, scanning, or otherwise without written permission from the publisher. It is illegal to copy this book, post it to a website, or distribute it by any other means without permission.

Special dedication to:
Trayvon Martin, Emmitt Till, Tony McDade, Oluwatoyin Salau,
Breonna Taylor, Rayshard Brooks, Amaud Arbery,
Sandra Bland, Mike Brown, Tamir Rice, the Charleston 9,
Amadou Diallo, Eric Garner, Philando Castile,
Dominique Clayton, Atatiana Jefferson,
Freddie Owens, Marcellus Willams,
and the many other souls
who were stripped from their bodies prematurely.

We honor you.

Table of Contents

Exhibit 1: Pre-Election Frenzy

These Are The Days 1
A Nice Nasty Message to the U.S. Government 5
The Pledge of Allegiance [Amended] 6
A Brief Interaction pt. II 7
Treefall 8
Disappointment 9
The Eagle 11
Superpower 18
Campaign Slogan 19

Exhibit 2: Remembering summer 2020

When the Lootin' Starts 23
How to Get Away With Murder 27
Go the Speed Limit 31
Ode to the Gift Shop Near the Entrance of the Cemetery 33

Exhibit 3: Post-Election Mayhem

Here's to Big Sister 41
In Pieces 42
Radically A Mess! 43
In Adam . . . Again 45
A Storm's Coming 47
Dear Mama 49
Creed for Success 53
The Stars Are Running At Us 54
Social Essay 56

About the Author 63

We shall meet in the place
where there is no darkness.

~ *George Orwell,* 1984

Summons
Poems + Photos

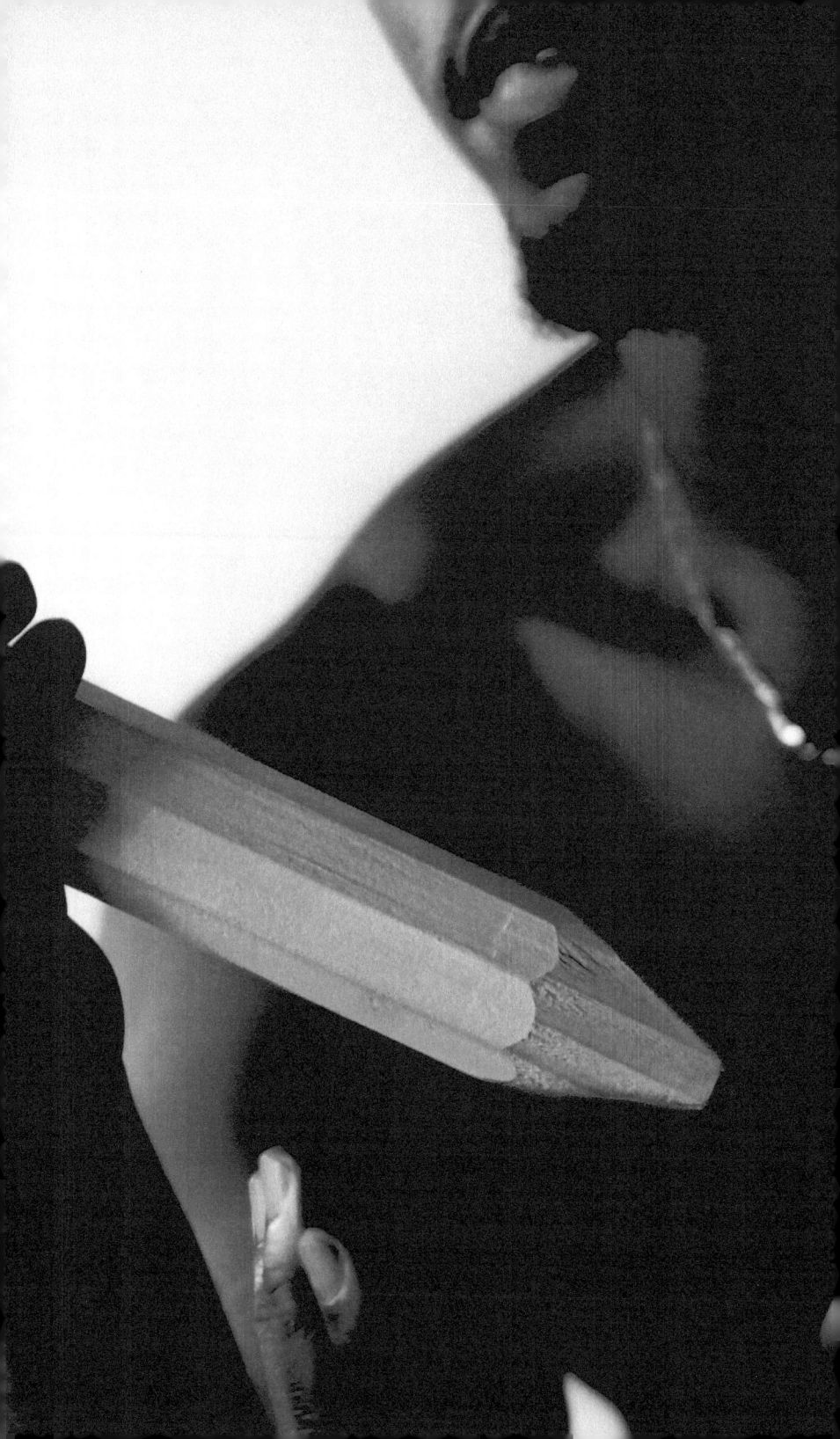

EXHIBIT 1:

Pre-Election Frenzy

"These Are The Days"

THESE ARE THE DAYS,
my friends,
where hypocrisy starts
and truth-seeking ends

where rent's past due,
landlords sue,
and bills so high
you could jump off a roof

bank accounts low,
seeds un-sowed,
working so hard
but have nothing to show

you lose your treasure once,
you'll lose it again
we lost before
we even knew to begin

a **stressed**, **depressed**,
& **work-obsessed** folk
who built the world with their souls
just to have it revoked

government officials
living lavish lifestyles
politician turned celebrity
shouldn't be allowed

democrat or influencer
both enamored by Hollywood
with policies on pause
as they try to cater to the hood

republican or bounty-men
both want your rights
with white christ in their corner,
it should be an easy fight

billionaires sink,
billionaires in space,
hoarding their wealth
is like a slap in the face

sell a little weed,
sell a little ass—
**we found a way
to rebuild the middle class**

tents go up,
tents go burn
homelessness is a crime
when will we ever learn

there's a ban on travel,
there's a ban on books,
there's a ban on the truth,
but immunity for crooks

it was their submission
that made our world go round,
sporting a mask
instead of wearing a frown

too proud to bend
and too poor to break,
we must push on
for our own namesake

there comes a time
when we must stand,
side by side,
hand in hand

change comes when we've
reached our bitter end
again, these are the days
indeed, my friends

"A Nice Nasty Message to the U.S. Government"

Bless your little heart.

"The Pledge of Allegiance [Amended]"

I pledge allegiance
to the ~~flag~~ **bill**,
of the ~~United~~ **Capitalist** States of America,
and ~~to the Republic~~ **in the shadows** for which it stands,
one Nation,
under ~~God~~ **Greed**,
~~in~~**divisible,**
with liberty and justice for ~~all~~ **...some.**

"A Brief Interaction pt. II"

Are you gonna vote?

No.

Bye.

"Treefall"

If a tree falls and there's no one around to witness it . . .

it still screams in agony.

"Disappointment"

Good food.
Good people.
Good vibes.

**They all
disappoint me.**

The wind
disappoints me,
and so does
my dad.

Apparently, I
should blame
the FBI
for that
& it makes
me want
to cry.

Will I ever be satisfied?
Perhaps.

Remember when
I told you
life would
go on?
Boy, was
I wrong.
Freedom is fading.

"The Eagle"

Once upon a midnight dreary,
while I pondered, all weak and weary,
over diplomatic fights on X,
and a potential civil war—

while I nodded, nearly napping,
exhausted from all the yapping,
something strange started happening,
as if someone was **tap, tap, tapping**
on my studio door.
"Who is this," I muttered,
"tapping on my studio door?"
Intrigued and nothing more.

Ah, distinctly I remember,
it was at the peak in November,
and one by one,
we brought ballots for a candidate to bestow.
Me? I eagerly longed for tomorrow,
where a lady I used to know,
here at our sea-washed, sunset gates,
would once again, lift her lamp
beside the golden door!
Now it feels
bleak, dark, and nothing more.

The thought of my suffrage filled me—
filled me with terrors never felt before;
And to calm the beating of my heart,
I stood repeating, "Who is that tapping on my studio door?"
Some unannounced, late night visitor.
This calls for the second amendment—now and forevermore!

Suddenly my will grew stronger;
hesitating then no longer,
"Sir," I said,
"or Madam, or They;
My rest awaits so you must go away.
Though gently you came
tap, tap, tapping,
at the time I was
nap, nap, napping,
alas, here we are at my studio door."
I brace myself to bare witness!
Opened the door with a quickness;
Darkness there and nothing more.

Deep into that Darkness peering,
I stood there slightly fearing—doubting
why I got up in the first place.
The silence remained unbroken;
the stillness, still eloping,
and the only word spoken came from me.
"Liberty?" I whispered,
and an echo murmured back, "Liberty!"
This, and nothing more.

Back into the studio I go,
my soul's been anchored, I know,
then came a louder tapping from across the way.
Let's see what happens! Let's see for the plot!
Is it the wind? Perhaps not.
I'll peek out the window to fully explore—
Again intrigued, but nothing more.

I opened the window
and in he swooped!
A handsome fellow
with eyes that drooped.

There stepped an Eagle
of the patriotic lore.
With honor and respect paid he.
Though an eerie sense gave he,
with avian privilege,
perched above my studio door—
Perched, pondered, and nothing more.

Then this proud bird
turned my worries over more,
emphasized by the bold and courageous fit he wore;
"Why are you so proud and fearless?
Are you aware of what you share?
Tell me what to call you when this country is in despair."
The Eagle says, "Justice."

I was shocked to hear this ungainly fowl,
to hear him answer all loud and proud;
though his answer had little meaning,
in a hurry, I started pleading,
"Why come tapping at my studio door?"
With such name as 'Justice,' his presence abhorred.

But the Eagle,
sitting alone on the frame of my door,
spoke only of his name,
nothing further, nothing more.
"Speak up!" I yell.
Repeat? Ought not!!
How does 'justice' explain
The disenfranchised?
The downtrodden?
The distraught?!!"
Ghosts of rights I've known before,
flew in as the beast went, "Justice"— and nothing more.

Startled at the stillness broken
by a reply so lamely spoken,
"Impossible," said I, "he repeats what he's heard—
A meaningless phrase from a meaningless bird."
But the Eagle, still enchanting,
turned my fancy into panting
as I pulled a chair close to the door;
Then upon my sitting,
I started overthinking
about this beast our founding fathers adored—
What did he mean by "justice?"
Was it here? Or lost at war? —
A game of lost and found, for sure!

Here I sat engaged and guessing.
No utterance made,
but my face? EXPRESSING.
Waiting for 'justice' to start addressing the inequality amongst the poor.
How gender crises intersect,
with **Black folx** disrespect,
I knew the Eagle was choosing to ignore.

Then the air grew thicker,
my rage, none quite quicker;
a new type of lynching to deplore.
"God!" said I, "or one of evil!—
Knowledge still, of divine or devil!
Tell me democracy's destiny!
Redeemable or haunted?
Though deserted its morals,
remains undaunted.
Is there peace in the Middle East?
How about in Memphis? LA?
"Justice," is all the bird had to say.

"That's that! It's time to go!
Only time will tell whether you were friend or foe!
Leave no trace of bird!
Leave my loneliness unbroken!—"
"Justice," said the Eagle,
Still, no other word spoken.

And the Eagle,
with no flutter,
still sitting on my shutter,
rested just above my door;
his eyes had all the seeming of a candidate still dreaming,
of a nation's birth, scheming
to make it great again,
though we swore
we never would.

So beware of the Eagle's flight,
coming in the break of night.
A sight rarely seen before;
and when the day is done,
and liberty's bell has rung,
we shall overcome
this, and forevermore!

"Superpower"

Controlling how I breathe will save me from this place.
My **superpower** will be my breath!

"Campaign Slogan"

WAR	IS	FUNDED.
FREEDOM	IS	LOVE.
IGNORANCE	IS	DEATH.

WAR IS FUNDED. FREEDOM IS LOVE.
IGNORANCE IS DEATH.

WAR IS FUNDED. FREEDOM IS LOVE. IGNORANCE IS... DEATH.

EXHIBIT 2:
Remembering Summer 2020

"When the Lootin' Starts"

the revolution becomes televised,
the headlines read "suicide,"
when both you and G*d
already know the truth
masters go swimming,
stores go burning,
and my mind wants revenge,
knowing that revenge
won't bring healing

say their names

when the lootin' starts,
I can't hear past
the harmonies
of my ancestors singing
"let freedom ring"
come to find out
freedom looked more like
a ring of fire
and the whole place
coming down in flames
I can't see past the smoke,
and I don't want to

they say they want
movers and shakers
until it's time
to shake some shit up

say their names

when the lootin' starts,
I can't leave my house
without a mask
protected from pigs
who throw teargas
in the middle of a pandemic

                                  COLD SHOWER
                                        after
                                  COLD SHOWER
                                        after
                                  COLD SHOWER
                       please, say their names

when the lootin' starts,
I find myself
walking a fine line
between
staying aware &
losing my sanity
until the line grows too thin
that I start to float

                                what strength comes
                                  from growing numb

I'm starting to think
they're the ones
crazed and dazed,
insane and inhumane,
evil and lame,
because things will
never be the same.

goddamnit,
say their names.

when the lootin' starts,
whites become
pick-mes
and talk about
"unprecedented times"
when all of this seems
so familiar
too familiar
black folk having
to resist
to exist

so what if the world seems
to be upside down
when my people
had to learn to walk on ceilings,
do the impossible,
just to live

SAY THEIR NAMES

when the lootin' starts,
I won't sit idly by
so I write for the voices
that'll never get to speak again
I write to illuminate
all of us
failed by the system

                                                                                  I **see** you
                                                                                  I **am** you

I'm screaming your name,
knowing that one day,
someone will stop,
listen,
and then scream with me

"How to Get Away With Murder"

**Welcome class! This is Criminal Law 100,
or as I prefer to call it: How to Get Away with Murder...
the easiest class to pass if you're a straight white man!**

Lesson 1: Be white. If you're not sure about one of your classmates, no problem! Check under your desk, where you'll find (drum roll, please)... The Scale of Morality! Anything from slight tan to "God, is there a single drop of melanin in you?" pale is fine. These shades will carry you to the promised land. But anything darker? Say, from buttercup to obsidian? We consider: a scumbag. When approaching scumbags, walk slowly. No eye contact! We can't have them thinking it's okay to be Black—next thing you know, they'll start multiplying. Clutch your pearls as tightly as possible, and call the police:

"Hello, 911? There's a... [Insert hard R word.... yes, that one.] walking the streets. How dare they!"

Lesson 2: Do not, under any circumstances, be queer. If you see a queer person—or God forbid, a group of them—take extreme caution! They might infect you with their "gay agenda." Solution? Buy a gun from your local Walmart and take them out—One. By. One. Don't worry! (As long as you're white... STRAIGHT and white.) We'll say you had a rough childhood—because who hasn't?

Lesson 3: Create barriers for anyone darker than white bread. Laws, policies, voting restrictions, you name it—use them like hurdles in a race where you're already miles ahead.

Lesson 4: Take this to memory: **She shouldn't have worn that.**

Lesson 5: (and this one, too) **"Racism, is over."**

Lesson 6: Cross-breed racism and sexism. Hell, cross all the -isms!

Lesson 7: Remember: "**-a**" in public, "**-er**" at home!

Lesson 8: Sprinkle in some confederate flags. You know, for heritage.

Lesson 9: Never forget: Daddy's money solves everything!

Finally, Lesson 10: remember what America was built on: taking from others, destroying families, and having others build the nation we love just to imprison and persecute them.

Class... welcome to How To Get Away With Murder, if you're who America was truly built for.

"Go the Speed Limit"

Sometimes my friends would complain
about getting pulled over
for speeding.
They'd laugh about getting
their latest ticket
and how they'd have
community service
this week and the next.

Then there's
the lucky ones
that could've gotten a ticket,
but the cop was cool.
All I can think is would that
"cool cop"
try to pull out his gun
if it were me?
Would my melanin become a sign saying
"shoot please"
and would I become another hashtag?

I'm terrified...
that what started out as a speeding ticket,
ended up being
an execution slip.
That when he told me,
"License and registration,"
It was a set up.
I've learned not to reach.
I've learned not to be belligerent.
I've learned that being complacent
wasn't an option either.

So no, sir.
My life is worth more
than what your badge
must think of me.
My life is worth so much more
than the 5 over I was going.

I understand –
"All cops aren't bad"
& you
"risk your lives everyday"
but try replacing
cops with black people.

All black people aren't bad.
We risk our lives everyday
just walking the streets
or selling CDs,
or reaching for that ID
that you so desperately want to see so…
here you go.

By the way,
Mr. Policeman,
Mr. Officer,
Mr. "Hero,"
You're supposed to have my back.
&
I know it's all
red,
white,
and **blue**…
but what about my **BLACK**?

"Ode to the Gift Shop Near the Entrance of the Cemetery"

Praise the closed caskets

Praise the cover
that conceals
that won't show the body
to the public—
or the bullet holes,
or the stains of whiteness

Praise the cops
who know that
their badge
grants clemency

Praise the untouched tasers

Praise the dark nights
of news untold before
white celebrities
can steal our movement

Praise the mother
in the gift shop
that can't stop wailing,
that's sick and tired

Praise the black people
who will never be free,
stuck following the slow progressions
of fabricated liberation
& systematic racism

Praise the healthcare system

Praise unemployment

Praise the poverty rate
& mass incarceration
& the friends we've lost
but have never forgotten

Praise the joggers
& the music blasters

Praise the corner store goers
& the kids who played cops and robbers

Praise the church goers
who were shipped on an
express to meet their Maker

Praise the ones that walk home
with skittles and
an Arizona

Praise the traffic tickets

Praise the reaching
though you were commanded to

Praise those who can't breathe,
who lie there
like they lay in their closed caskets

Praise the restless souls
the tired souls that are sick and tired of being sick and tired

Praise those who are tired
of all of this mess.

EXHIBIT 3:

Post-Election Mayhem

"Here's to Big Sister"

In **1984**, there was Big Brother.
In **2024**, we could've had Big Sister.

                                        Same daddy, different mama.
                                            She put up a good fight.

"In Pieces"

> We only yearned to live in peace,
> not pieces.

"Radically A Mess!"

I was never really radical . . .
except when someone told me I couldn't do something.

"In Adam . . . Again"

Bang!
Bang!!
Bang!!!
Total chaos (~~total bliss~~)

IN ADAM,
there's a new kind of fruit.
Strange and eerie—
Poisoned from the root.

IN ADAM,
autumn brings
lynch-stained leaves,
and bodies still swing from sycamore trees.

IN ADAM,
we knew that this was the outcome, too.
To be led by green,
rather than red or blue.

We yell, "I hate this place!!" until Olympic day,
and then patriots we became.
Social delusion so clearly constructed
to blind us from the shame.

IN ADAM,
there's no separation between church and state.

IN ADAM,
there's no right to choose.

Here,
our morals are compromised
by the fruit we once refused.

IN ADAM,
the human condition worsens
as we survive this present hell.
Living lives too terrifying to see beyond the veil.

A deranged fruit.
A stained fruit.
We pluck them
one by one.

IN ADAM,
we grieve
knowing that
the feast has just begun.

"A Storm's Coming"

It's warm.
Almost enough for a sweat.
I sweat too easily.
The breeze cools me just enough.
The birds are...
chirping or arguing?
Who the hell knows.
These blood suckers.
Irritating.
I got bit again.
The air has a certain stickiness.
I'm sweating.
Big daddy complains.
It's a slow day.
A calm one.
A storm's coming.
He can feel it in his knee.
We get up.
Car's packed.
I left my hat.
Reverse.
That's where I saw him.
Small body.
Big heart.
A little black guy.
Like me.
Struggling to carry his load.
Where is he going?
I can kill him.
Who would ever know?
Bastard.
I don't.

He's gone.
It's beautiful.
The orange.
The magenta.
The plum.
The deep, deep blue.
The dark.
The grey.

It rains.

"Dear Mama"

I want to be like the sun, unafraid to shine bright,
I want to be like the moon, guarding you through the night.

I want to be like the clouds, drifting free in the air,
Light and calm, without worry or care.

I want to be like the sea, deep, powerful, and strong,
Carrying the strength you've shown me all along.

I want to be the joke that always makes you smile,
I want to be the peaceful nap you'd take for a while.

I want to dream big and be free to fall,
Free to make my mistakes and still stand tall.

I want to walk the streets with my head held high,
Without fear that my worth will be denied.

I want to love my skin and be proud to be Black,
To beat the odds, and then give back.

I want to thrive in a world not built for me,
And learn to write my own destiny.

To push the limits, though the world says no.
My strength is more than they'll ever know.

Strong enough to do, wise enough to be,
Thank you for the example you've set for me.

Thank you for all that you've done and still do.

I love you,
I love you,
I LOVE YOU!

In admiration,
Your son

"Creed for Success"

Today,
I will be the best that I can be.
I will do the best that I can do.
I will change those things that stop my success
and accept those things that I cannot change
because they are for my best!
I am cheerfully and wonderfully made.
My dreams for success? I will not let fade.
I must follow my personal rules.
I WILL BE SUCESSFUL
because
I remain a student of life!
I remain open to the lessons the world has
to teach me.

"The Stars are Running at Us"

In the presence of nature,
we all become children again.
So if you can't stop to witness the colors,
or the stars,
then what's the point?

Our memories are the best we have—
until they start to fade, too.
We recall the colors
until we can't.

> The burnt oranges.
> The passionate violets.
> The banded blues.

We will worry
of tomorrow
in due time,
but today
must be lived and celebrated!

> Chase the fire!
> Isn't that neat?

The stars are running at us!
Showing how the meaning of life
lies in awe,
rubbing its belly,
eyes closed—
fulfilled.

The journey we took together
was everything.

"Social Essay"

I take public transportation... a lot. It's a love-hate relationship. I hate the smell and how dirty it is, but I love how (for the most part) it's free. Cheers to all the times we've used a simple "good morning" as payment on the bus, and here's to tipping with a smile and a "thank you!" Shoutout to the bus driver who drives the 204 local like it's the 754 rapid. You've single-handedly taught me two things:
1) **We do not exist without a village, and**
2) **Life remains the biggest classroom... especially when you're running late.**

After a transfer or two, I'd arrive at school and step into one of my most important roles: Mr. Moore, an elementary school teacher. One of the biggest lessons I teach is **resiliency**. Kids can comprehend more than we give them credit for. For example, they knew about my hour commute, about how I had to take at least two buses to get there. They knew I was committed to showing up for them—something that wasn't easy, but it was a choice. They knew that they were chosen. I loved how chosen they feel.

So, I'd go through my day teaching, facilitating, diffusing, and breathing. [I had to find moments to breathe.] Somehow, the day would end, and it'd be time to head to the train station.

When I got there, I'd realize just how spent I was and just how much of myself I had given. I'd sigh—time to make the trek home. Soon enough, I'd hear "Train to Union Station" come over the speakers, and I'd watch as everyone around me seem just as tired. We had all overextended ourselves in ways no one could imagine. Everyone would rather order an Uber if they could afford it. See, resiliency was teaching me that it comes in many forms, **but humility** was showing me that just beyond my ego was a way to save a lot of money!

Moments later, the train doors would open, and boom—clothes on the floor. I'm used to it now. The displaced garments and the remnants of food. The smell of pee: both animal and human. I could tell someone had been there, and God help them if this was their best option for the night.

I'd get on, head on a swivel, because while I come in peace, you won't catch me slippin'. As I sit down, a man walks in. His clothes were worn and ripped, riddled with stains, but his head remained high. His chest? Out. There was a bit of swagger in his shoulders as he picked up his belongings and left. In my head, I thought, "Good for him," and then remembered that video of the cleaner trains in China. Meanwhile, here I am in dirty ol' LA, on a train that felt like both a burden and a blessing. Shoutout to the oxymorons of life—the things that shouldn't make sense but do.

Shoutout to God, the greatest teacher, and shoutout to Chicago Bill, who I'd run into on my way home. He'd always remind me that my accent is a part of me, no matter how hard I tried to mask it, and how I should always be laughing because of my "million-dollar smile." (There's a message in there somewhere.)

At this point, it was obvious he was buttering me up, hoping I'd buy him something. I let him butter me up anyway—after all, I'm from the south and I do love butter! Plus, I had already made up my mind when I saw him: two bananas and an Electrolit.

Chicago Bill has always been a part of my story, and me a part of his. The Metro system has always been a part of my story, and vice versa. Even if it's brief, when we reach out and touch someone, we help propel them towards their destiny. The village depends on it. I depend on it. So, thank you.

To my tribe: I need you now more than ever.

About the Author

Marquavious Moore was born and raised in Memphis, TN, where the rich, cultural landscape helped shape his artistic voice. Moore studied Psychology and African American and African Diaspora Studies at Columbia University, combining his passion for understanding the human mind with a deep commitment to exploring Black history and identity.

His poetry has garnered recognition by the National Civil Rights Museum for his work addressing issues of injustice, heritage, and community. In 2017, he was named Tennessee's Poetry Out Loud champion.

Summons is his second self-published poetry collection, continuing his journey of using art to confront societal challenges and celebrate the resilience of Black life.

Website: MarquaviousMoore.com
Instagram/X/Tiktok: @MDMoore_

www.ingramcontent.com/pod-product-compliance
Lightning Source LLC
Chambersburg PA
CBHW020244010526
44107CB00002B/95